Anchored in Purpose

Positioning Yourself for a Fulfilling Life

JEWEL BRODIE-REID

Anchored in Purpose: Positioning Yourself for a Fulfilling Life

© 2016 Jewel Brodie-Reid. All rights reserved. No part of this book may be reproduced, stored in a retrieval system, or transmitted by any means, except for brief quotations in printed reviews, without the written permission of Jewel Brodie-Reid. Requests may be submitted by email: Jewel@TheGemInYou.com.

ISBN: 978-0-9977893-0-0

Published by Javery Group Publishing 2016

All Scripture quotations, unless otherwise noted, are taken from the New King James Version. Copyright © 1982 by Thomas Nelson, Inc. Used by permission. All rights reserved.

Scripture passages marked "KJV" are from the King James Version. Public domain.

Because of the Internet's dynamic nature, any web addresses or links contained within this book may have changed since publication or prove no longer valid.

*To those searching for fulfillment,
may you discover God's purpose
for your life.*

We know that all things work together for good to them that love God, to them who are the called according to his purpose.

Romans 8:28 KJV

Contents

Acknowledgments vii

Introduction.. ix

Chapter 1: The Relationship between
  God, Creation, Vision, and Purpose 1

Chapter 2: Getting Started
  (Compass Principles 1–2) 9

Chapter 3: Identifying Strengths
  (Compass Principles 3–5) 17

Chapter 4: Removing Hindrances
  (Compass Principle 6) 25

Chapter 5: Making a Plan and Executing It
  (Compass Principles 7–10) 31

Notes 45

For Further Reading 46

About the Author 47

Acknowledgments

As I add my final touches to this book, I'm deeply aware that credit for its completion goes first to God. Thank you, Lord, for equipping me with spiritual gifts and talents that enabled me to write this Life Purpose Coaching workbook. You've blessed me with knowledge, wisdom, and insights that can help people discover the purposes you designed for their lives.

I am also grateful for my husband, James Reid. Thank you for loving me unconditionally and showing me patience. You've always encouraged me and supported my dreams. Thanks for compelling me to complete this book with a spirit of excellence.

Gwendolyn Brodie, my mother, thanks for loving and providing for me despite life's challenges. You taught me to never give up. Thank you for always believing me capable of accomplishing anything I set my mind to conquer.

Sophia Brodie, my grandmother, you are the heart of who I am. Your unwavering love, courage, and strength have always inspired me. Thank you for being one of the most influential Christian women in my life. I'm grateful for the many treasured moments we've shared.

And finally, I say thanks to my late Uncle LB. You exemplified what it means to live a Christ-centered life. You always demonstrated what it looks like to love and support your spouse with all your heart. I am so grateful you showed me the importance of leaving a godly legacy for generations to come.

Introduction

Do you ever wonder what you were born to do?

Do you dread getting up tomorrow to go to a job for which you have no passion?

Do you feel trapped by circumstances that keep you from living out your dreams?

If so, you're missing out on a purposeful life.

Living a life of purpose happens when you work or volunteer in a field about which you are truly passionate. Doing so maximizes the use of your God-given gifts and talents and drives you to excel beyond the norm. Those who live purposefully derive immense fulfillment from what they do and are often amazed at the positive impact they're able to make on others. You too can experience this!

All of us were created for a godly purpose. Ephesians 2:10 explains that you and I are God's "workmanship," the Lord's masterpieces. The verse goes on to clarify that we are individuals "created in Christ Jesus" to do the "good works" he planned specifically for us to accomplish. We were made to glorify God by utilizing the gifts and talents entrusted to us.

This is not a one-size-fits-all assignment. Think about it. There is something within you that sets you apart from everyone else: you've got talents and dreams and passions that are all your own. In addition to blessing you with these, God has equipped you with the skills to persevere, overcome, and effectively operate in using those things for his glory as you live out his plans for your life. For some, the kind of purposeful living I'm talking about might involve starting a new business that meets specific needs like helping others with debt management and career development. For others, it might mean utilizing counseling skills to help victims of domestic violence. Still others may find their greatest joy and satisfaction in raising children who love the Lord. The possibilities are endless, diverse, and wonderful.

It's time to ask whether you are ready to seek change and to make changes. Are you willing to do what God has called you to do?

If you will dedicate time, energy, and resources to bring God glory, you will find a purposeful life. You can indeed engage in work that brings you such contentment that you can't even call it work! So if you're up to the challenge of seeing your life transformed, let's take a journey to discover your unique purpose.

Chapter 1
The Relationship between God, Creation, Vision, and Purpose

This book's message of how Christians might position themselves to live in such a way that they feel anchored to a divine purpose is one I first discovered within the Holy Bible. Christians accept the Bible as a true account of Creator God's dealings with the world. It teaches why we were made, why work is often difficult, and why suffering exists; and it helps us to know how to live in spite of hurdles. It also gives secrets for life success like this one: "Meditate in [Scripture] day and night, that you may observe to do according to all that is written in it. For then you will make your way prosperous, and then you will have good success" (Joshua 1:8). It's my conviction, then, that only within the Bible will we find the keys for living out our fullest potential.

To grasp how to live on purpose, we must first understand the relationship of Creation, Vision, and Purpose, noting how each element is connected to God. This idea is based on scriptural teachings and is illustrated in the Purpose Pyramid on the following page.

The Purpose Pyramid

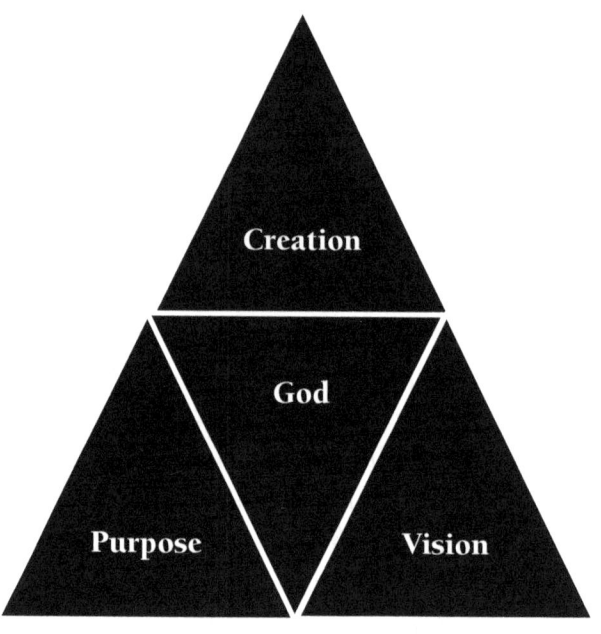

1. Understand why you were created.

The following biblical passage illustrates the first aspect of the Purpose Pyramid. In Jeremiah 1:5, God the Creator said, "Before I formed you in the womb I knew you; Before you were born I sanctified you; I ordained you a prophet to the nations."

All individuals are created by God and bear his image. Of interest here is that God ordained Jeremiah's life purpose *prior to his conception*. God called him to be a prophet—one who served not only the inhabitants of Judah but also neighboring nations. In the same manner in which God decreed Jeremiah's purpose, God has assigned you a purpose too.

Perhaps you are wondering how to identify what it is you were created to do. How do you find that path of divine purpose in which your days can be filled with contentment rather than the frustrations of just another day in the office?

Finding answers requires an understanding of one of the most universal elements of God's plan for us: he desires that we have an intimate relationship with him. God wants us to know him. He wants us to speak to him and listen for his direction. As surely as he walked and talked with the first couple, Adam and Eve, in the cool of the day, God desires to be an integral part of our lives (Genesis 3:8).

Having a close relationship with God seems a simple matter, but the truth is that many of us fail to seek and maintain a strong and engaging relationship with him. Instead, our involvement with the Lord is occasional at best. We may, for instance, pray from time to time, but we tend to call on him only when we want something or are in serious trouble. What we need is true intimacy, and that requires constant prayer and a steady delight in God's Word, regardless of whether we're enjoying the highs of life or tumbling down valleys of disappointment. Finding our purpose and living in it can never be realized until we diligently seek and maintain that intimate relationship with God.

Before we go further, we must understand there is but one means through which we can enjoy that intimate connection with God, and that is through Jesus Christ.

Since the time Adam and Eve did the one thing God asked them not to do, humanity's perfect fellowship with God has been broken by sin (see Genesis 3). Our sin problem, understood as the wrongs we do, leads to all kinds of trouble for us in this life and robs us of eternal life. Sin's presence in the world, in fact, is why we die (Romans 6:23).

But God's love for us is so great that he allowed his only Son, Jesus Christ, to die on the cross as a sacrifice that could satisfy his righteous wrath against our wrongs. In John 14:6, Jesus said, "I am the way, the truth, and the life. No one comes to the Father except through Me." You see, throughout his earthly lifetime, Jesus knew he was coming to take the punishment we deserved. In giving up his life for ours, Christ saw that all who would repent and place faith in him as Savior would be saved from God's anger against our sin. And it gets better! Three days later he was raised to life again, reminding us that those who accept Jesus as Lord aren't just forgiven in God's eyes. They too will live again, eternally, in a fabulous place called heaven. And in the meantime, we have Christ's help to live abundantly today (John 10:10).

What we do with Jesus Christ is important: he is *the key* to purposeful living. He's the Wonderful Counselor and the Prince of Peace (Isaiah 9:6). So, if you haven't accepted him as your Savior, consider the truth of Romans 10:9: "If you confess with your mouth the Lord Jesus and believe in your heart that God has raised Him from the dead, you will be saved."

I focus on this topic not simply because I believe it is such a critical matter but because accepting Jesus really does open the door for intimacy with our Creator. Those who accept Christ can go to God in prayer with "boldness," knowing they have "access" to him (Ephesians 3:12). And what a great gift that is as we seek to live out the purposes he designed for us! Only when we have a relationship with God through Jesus Christ and begin seeking him through prayer can we grasp that he created us with gifts and talents to be used to serve others.

We often think about gifts and talents in terms of gaining fame or making money, but God doesn't bless us just to enrich ourselves or make our names great. Rather, he designed us with specific gifts to meet specific needs. For example, perhaps you have the gift of patience and a talent for nursing. If so, you may have been created to comfort or care for the homeless, elderly, or ill. Or it could be that you have a knack for encouragement and are a skilled teacher. If so, maybe you were made to train and encourage others as they develop professionally or spiritually. Gifts and talents are many and varied. The point is that all of us have strengths, talents, or skills that can be used to make the world a better place.

Isn't it wonderful to know that God created each of us with a specific purpose in mind? We need never face another purposeless day again.

2. Visualize God's plan for your life.

Proverbs 29:18 illustrates the second element of the Purpose Pyramid. It states, "Where there is no vision, the people perish" (KJV). In other words, living a purposeful life requires that we each function with an overarching sense of direction. We should ask, "Where am I going, and how am I going to get there?"

For those who follow Christ, our end destination is heaven. We'll get there because we placed faith in what Jesus did for us on the cross. But in the meantime, we can live with the goal of living out our potential in him, seeking to understand and follow his plans for us.

God's vision for our lives often exceeds what we can imagine. You might see yourself helping at a homeless shelter, for instance, while God's vision for your life involves you *opening* a homeless shelter. You might picture yourself volunteering in church ministry (as I once did), never guessing that over time God will prompt your heart to *lead* various ministries and even to teach classes. Yes, it could be that God has something totally different in mind from the future you see for yourself.

So often, due to self-inflicted limitations, people struggle with visualizing God's plan. They get so discouraged by past experiences, a lack of knowledge and skills, or a lack of money or time that they just assume achieving God's best for them is hopeless. *There's no way I can do that,* some might think. *I'm not qualified to do that.*

But what we fail to realize is that if God has ignited a passion and desire in us and if we are willing to seek him in prayer and obedience, he will make certain we have the knowledge, skills, and resources to live out his plans. With his love, power, and blessings at work on your behalf, you can overcome even the highest barriers and embrace opportunities you have yet to see coming.

3. Commit to purposeful living.

Romans 8:28 sheds light on the third element of the Purpose Pyramid. It says, "We know that all things work together for good to them who love God, to them who are the called according to His purpose" (KJV). Within that statement there is a sense of mission and certainty that should change the way we live: if we are walking in relationship with God, we can know that he will weave all the threads of our experiences into something good, something beautiful.

This Scripture speaks to God's wonderful grace, which allows us to be forgiven of our sins. It also highlights the miraculous way he can use all of our experiences for good if we simply obey him. Despite your past mistakes, negative influences you've endured, or the trials and tribulations that have come your way, your love of God puts you in a position to see him use such hardships for good.

Let me share a story that illustrates how this principle worked in my life. One of my greatest hardships as an adult was getting laid off. When it happened, I only saw the financial implications, the mental stress, and the negative stigma of being unemployed. But today, looking back, I realize that being laid off gave me the opportunity to pursue a career in a different industry. It was in that season that I grasped the importance of networking, something I had never really valued before. I learned how to nurture professional connections and tap into executive search firms and online career centers. And today, that's the very kind of career assistance I provide to clients and associates when they come to me seeking advice.

Don't let past mistakes or disappointments make you think that purposeful living is for others but not for you. Decide today to get on track, living out whatever it is God would have you do. Ask him to give you wisdom to make better decisions—to give you the courage to turn failures into testimonies that help others stay on track. All of your life experiences make up your unique purpose, so don't overemphasize past hardships. Trials and tribulations strengthen our emotional and mental resolve. Allow God to work through them.

Chapter 2

Getting Started
(Compass Principles 1–2)

Now that we reviewed the Purpose Pyramid and how it applies to purposeful living, let's take a look at what I call **Compass Principles**, ten sequential steps I've created with your success in mind. I want to partner with you in the task of anchoring your life to God's plans, and I believe that following these steps will prove crucial as you navigate to the harbor of a purpose-filled life.

1. Assess Where You Are (Do a Reality Check)
2. Establish Your Spiritual Foundation
3. Identify Your Passions
4. Identify Your Spiritual Gifts and Talents
5. Identify Your Opportunity Areas (Do an Opportunity Check)
6. Identify Your Destiny Blockers (Do a Barrier Check)
7. Determine Where You Should Be (Do a Dream Check)
8. Create an Action Plan
9. Embrace Purposeful Mentorship
10. Take the First Step

In the pages ahead, I aim to steer you down a channel that might well lead to the meaningful life you've been craving. But know that this journey may be difficult and filled with obstacles, distractions, and discouraging words from naysayers. But if you remain steadfast, you'll reach a beautiful destination and will no doubt reap unforeseen rewards.

God has a plan for *your* life. He knows your beginning and

your end. So commit to this time of self-exploration and allow me to partner with you along the way.

In this chapter we'll discuss the first two Compass Principles.

Compass Principle 1:
Assess Where You Are (Do a Reality Check)

The journey to your future requires that you first conduct a reality check. Simply ask yourself whether you are living a purposeful life. And answer candidly.

If you find it difficult to respond to that question, think about the past year up until today. How has your life progressed? How has your career progressed? Are you fulfilled? Are you motivated? Are you happy with your current state of affairs? Wrestling with these matters can help you determine if you are where you desire to be.

Write today's date and your self-assessment thoughts here:

_____

_____

_____

_____

Perhaps this exercise helped you see that your life is progressing in just the direction you aim to go. If so, that's terrific! But it could also be that doing the reality check led to a wave of discouragement. If so, don't despair. Realizing that something is broken is the first step to repairing it.

On the following pages are two reality checks I completed in 2012. Notice the change in tone that took place between January and June. You'll see that some course corrections were made in the months between the two assessments.

January 5

Last year was a series of peaks and valleys. After being in a position for over three years, I was hired in a new internal position as a Corporate Director. This was an exciting opportunity that allowed me to flourish! I got the opportunity to define key customer satisfaction metrics, I helped define and standardize processes for the entire organization, and my manager often asked for my insight on various improvement initiatives. I truly felt valued as an employee.

But all those achievements didn't prevent me from being a part of the annual cost cutting strategy. Management decided that my role could be filled less expensively by two junior-level roles. The result was yet another layoff! I can't believe that happened to me again! How did I go from a high-performer to the unemployment office?

I'm disappointed and discouraged. I'm angry. I'm mentally drained. And I'm not sure whether I'm living a purposeful life or not. (God, how do I move forward from here? Why is this happening to me? What are you trying to tell me? Is there another path that you want me to pursue?)

June 4

This year I experienced a pivotal milestone in my life. I turned forty. Turning forty isn't the easiest thing to accept because I feel like half of my life is over. I can't believe I've been on the planet for four decades! However, when I assess my life, I can honestly say that I'm in a good place.

Despite the highs and lows, my relationship with God continues to grow and develop. And I now have a fundamen-

tal understanding of my purpose. Oddly, I think it's all the job upheaval I wrote about at the start of the year that helped me see it. (God, I truly believe that you never want me to get comfortable in a corporate job. You want me to gain plenty of knowledge and insight from various work experiences and industries so that I can help others make better career decisions—no matter their background.)

Every obstacle I overcome gives me the tools to help others. Every test I encounter gives me a testimony. Every failure I endure becomes a catalyst for self-improvement. I'm very much a work in progress, but I'm committed to aligning my life to God's Word. I like what I'm doing, and I feel like I'm on track.

Did you notice how my perspective changed between the two reality checks? In January, I was focused on my disappointments. I had almost drowned in a whirlpool of self-pity. However, by June, my attitude shifted. Why? Because I focused on growing my relationship with God, and as I made that change, I also gained a better understanding of my purpose. Though I had achieved corporate success, God was using my negative experiences—like those layoffs—as a training ground for my future in Life Coaching.

Maybe you are weighing my story against your own and worry that your present situation is so far from your dreams or goals that you'll never get where you want to go. Maybe you aren't just in an unfulfilling career but are also involved in something you know does not align with God's desires for you.

If so, reflect on Romans 8:28 and remind yourself that "all things work together for good to them that love God, to them who are called according to his purpose" (KJV). (And if you are caught up in habits or choices that run contrary to God's Word, repent and start living in obedience to Christ.) Also, be willing to seek resources such as motivational seminars, counseling, life groups, or coaching to help you move forward. And never lose sight of the value of surrounding yourself with positive influences. Positive words promote positive outcomes.

No matter how you answered the assessment, I challenge you to be on the lookout for a peer whom you think would say, "I am right where I believe God wants me in life, and I am doing exactly what he would have me do." While it's rare to find someone who genuinely loves his or her career and believes it aligns to his or her passions and purpose, I can't overstate the encouragement we can find in listening to the stories of a person like that. I encourage you to invite such a person out for coffee this week to find out how he or she was able to achieve such a meaningful and rewarding life path.

Compass Principle 2: Establish Your Spiritual Foundation

Once you've assessed your current situation, it's time to strengthen (or establish) a spiritual foundation on which you can rely in the days ahead. If you've accepted Christ as your Savior, you never have to walk through life alone. But having a spiritual foundation means more than just knowing you belong to God. It means you allow your belief in him to serve as the basis or groundwork for anything you do. It means you make him your ultimate life anchor.

Having a spiritual foundation means allowing God's rules and desires for his children to influence our lives. It means that we obey the Ten Commandments and treat others as we would like to be treated. It means that pleasing him is our highest aim. But we won't know God's commands or understand how he wants us to live unless we spend time with him.

If you are unsure about the strength of your spiritual foundation, consider your level of intimacy with God. Ask yourself the following questions:

1. How often do I pray?

_____

_____

2. When do I pray? When things are bad or at all times?

_____

_____

3. What types of things do I share with God?

_____

_____

4. How do I show affection to God?

_____

_____

5. How often do I seek God's Word for guidance and insight?

_____

_____

6. How often do I thank him for *all* blessings?

_____

_____

7. How often do I read God's Word in a typical week?

_____

_____

8. In what areas do I actually apply God's Word?

_____

_____

Intimacy with God requires constant prayer and the reading of his Word. Based on your responses, what do you need to do to strengthen your spiritual foundation?

_____

_____

We normally think about relationships in terms of our connections with our parents, children, spouses, significant others, or close friends, but the same rules by which we gauge the health of those relationships also apply to our connection with God. Think about it. Intimacy is often measured by frequency of communication, familiarity, the depth of things shared between two parties, and tangible acts or expressions of love.

The more grounded in and intimate you are with Christ, the

more likely you will stay on course during your journey to purposeful living. So if you can't remember the last time you told God how much you loved him, aren't sure when you last dedicated distraction-free time to pray and draw closer to God, or have no idea when you last read God's Word, it's time to make some changes. You've got to seal the cracks in your spiritual foundation.

Please recognize that personal time, errands, and your career are less important than pursuing a healthy, vibrant relationship with your Creator. Because, friend, if you want to move forward and desire to live out your potential, you will need his help. As Proverbs 16:9 states, "A man's heart plans his way, but the Lord directs his steps."

Chapter 3

Identifying Strengths
(Compass Principles 3–5)

You've assessed your current situation and you've considered ways to strengthen your spiritual foundation. You are well into your journey toward a deeper sense of purposefulness. The next step is to take inventory of your strengths and to consider areas in which you may need to improve.

Compass Principle 3:
Identify Your Passions

This stop on your journey involves identifying your passions. For what subject or activity do you have deep interest or strong enthusiasm? Identifying your passions is a critical part of living a purposeful life because our healthy interests are often closely linked to the purposes God has for us.

Traveling is one of my passions, and it is an integral part of my work as a Life Coach. I love visiting new countries, meeting new friends, and enjoying delicious, exotic cuisine. I get so excited anticipating these things that I often can't sleep the nights prior to my trips. But I hadn't always enjoyed an opportunity to indulge those interests. I just knew it was something I'd love to do.

Growing up with a limited income in rural North Carolina meant spending my childhood daydreaming about traveling to faraway lands rather than visiting them. But during a college internship, I got my first opportunity to travel by plane. Excited and nervous, I flew to Rochester, New York. It was the farthest I had traveled from home. The experience made me eager for new chances to fly. I was hooked!

Since that first adventure, I've visited multiple countries and traveled all over the United States to teach, train, and coach others on the use of a systematic method to attain desired goals. And you know what? Without my built-in love for traveling, I'd find it mighty difficult to do my job. You see, when the Lord gave me a passion for sightseeing and venturing to new places, he knew what he was doing. He was prepping me to live out the life purpose he designed for me. (And I'm thankful to report that he blessed me with a husband who loves travel as much as I do!)

Below are a few examples of common passions, specific areas of interest that the Lord places within his people in preparation for the work he would have them do. Circle all the items on the list that appeal to you.

Passions Chart

- Health and Fitness
- Professional Success
- Connecting People & Ideas
- Learning
- Traveling
- Writing
- Motivating Others
- Mentoring
- Outreach
- Missions
- Poverty
- Discipleship
- Youth
- Teaching
- Leading Others
- Giving

Allow yourself to dream. For what jobs or experiences might the Lord have intended to prepare you when he gave you such interests?

_____

_____

Compass Principle 4
Identify Your Spiritual Gifts and Talents

The fourth stop on your journey builds on Compass Principle 3. It's at this point that you need to consider and identify your talents. God has granted each of us special strengths and abilities with which we can work and be a blessing. It's important for us to know what these talents are because utilizing them is *essential* if we are to live up to our potential.

My dominant gifts are leadership, administration, encouraging, writing, critical thinking, and problem solving. Some of these, like the talent for critical thinking, I was unaware of until adulthood. I slowly realized that ability after I found myself constantly calculating methods to improve process performance and wait times while standing in airport security lines. And when my car's dashboard began to fade after less than two years, I was obsessed with determining the causes of the defect, going so far as to study the impact of heat, humidity, and ultraviolet light on various materials. Eventually I recognized that analyzing comes naturally for me.

Other talents, such as writing, have been obvious to me since childhood. For instance, back in grade school, I dismissed the standard recommendation of writing essays by creating an outline before drafting the essay. Instead, I would just write the essay. The result was always an A. I didn't need an outline. It was easy for me to weave words into a compelling story.

Admittedly, some of my talents would have remained dormant had they not developed through my life experiences. Throughout my professional career, I served in roles in which I led and managed projects. Leading such projects requires great time management and administrative skill. As my career progressed, my leadership roles transitioned into those that required me to coach managers and leaders to drive business results. From this work came a love of seeing individuals grow and develop professionally and personally.

One way to identify your talents—those that are a part of your life today and those that may be waiting to shine in your future—is to think about the things you do well. On what activities are you often complimented? What things come easily to you? In what situations do people frequently ask for your help or advice?

Below is an abbreviated list of talents. Circle those you believe you have. Place a question mark beside those you suspect you have but may need to nurture. Feel free to identify others not listed.

Gifts and Talents Chart

- Administration
- Evangelism
- Faith
- Pastoral
- Singing
- Writing
- Music
- Public Speaking
- Humor

- Apostleship
- Encouraging
- Leadership
- Teaching
- Dancing
- Drawing
- Acting
- Critical Thinking
- Future Thinking

If you answered that last activity with a lot of question marks, consider asking close friends or trusted coworkers for their insight. Sometimes, others can see our gifts more clearly than we can. You must be open to receiving feedback regarding your talents. Don't second-guess or discount people who point out a gift you don't think you have, and don't get upset with those who fail to think you are as strong at a particular talent as you believe.

Over the years, I've received a lot of valuable insight from coworkers and friends. I received multiple corporate awards and recognition for projects that I led, managed, or coached. Even before I began my career, people would often come to me for advice and encouragement about their professional and personal lives. Little did I know that all of these things were preparing me for my calling as a Life Purpose Coach®; it's a role in which I can help individuals identify their unique purposes in Christ.

Even with the feedback from friends or coworkers, be in continual prayer regarding your gifts. Know that some talents will be utilized more than others depending on the season of your life. Seek God daily so that your gifts can be recognized and maximized for his glory.

Also remain aware that sometimes we must overcome barriers in order to use our natural talents. It's well known that as a child, James Earl Jones—a gifted actor and the voice of Darth Vader—had a severe stuttering problem.[1] I'm sure he was teased mercilessly by some of his peers. Yet he grew up to thrill audiences worldwide with the rich timbre of his voice. Surely, somewhere along the way, someone encouraged him to overcome his stuttering and told him that he might one day be well-known for his tone. So listen for voices of encouragement, and be willing to nurture gifts you've yet to embrace.

Whatever your talents are, they can be used for God's glory, for your good, and for meeting others' needs. Don't be shy about identifying and using them.

Importantly, a dominant professional gift or talent does not always equate to a dominant spiritual gift, which one theologian describes as "the special abilities with which the Holy Spirit empowers us as we work within our churches."[2] Just because you are a great corporate leader does not mean you need to assume a leadership role in church. Sometimes, good professional leaders can make the greatest contribution to the body of Christ (the church) by performing acts of service. I served in hospitality ministry and mentored young girls for many years before becoming a Life Purpose Coach®.

To identify your spiritual gifts, consider taking a spiritual gift assessment test. These tests, available online, help people discover their abilities and find meaningful ways to use them in conjunction with supporting the work of the local church.[3] Once you take the assessment, take a moment to review the results and determine how your gifts might contribute to your unique purpose. Be aware that assessment results may change over time if you take multiple tests, so look at your results as dynamic indicators of your gifts during your life's journey.

Compass Principle 5:
Identify Your Opportunity Areas (Do an Opportunity Check)

The fifth stop on your journey may prove one of the most challenging: it's at this point that you must pause to identify your Opportunity Areas. That's a nice way of saying that it's time to take note of your weaknesses.

By using the term "weaknesses," I'm not referring to deep-seated character flaws or sinful tendencies. Rather, the goal of the current Compass Principle is simply to help you identify areas in which you may need further improvement, development, and growth before reaching your potential and living out your God-given purpose with confidence.

Below are some common Opportunity Areas. Underline those that describe concerns that may hinder you. Think of activities on your job that you dislike. What tasks make you feel uncomfortable? Which are difficult for you to do despite repetition? Often the answers will help you identify underlying weaknesses.

Opportunity Areas

- lack of a certain skill
- lack of resources
- lack of financial knowledge
- lack of leadership skills
- lack of creativity
- poor time management skills
- lack of business acumen
- inability to trust others
- inability to engage others
- inability to multi-task
- inflexibility
- poor writing skills

Frankly, I have several opportunity areas. At times, I find it difficult to trust others to complete projects in which I'm actively involved. And because I'm so analytical and systematic, I can be inflexible.

The good news is that because I'm aware of these issues, I can make a conscious effort to overcome deficiencies by using various resources. If I need creative input, for instance, I solicit feedback from a creative friend or source. When I'm working with others, I give project insight and guidance, but deliberately step away to allow them to complete projects in the manner that's most effective for them. I'm still working on becoming more flexible. Because my natural make-up is that of a critical thinker, it's difficult for me to conceptualize ideas or recommendations that aren't backed by data. However, I recognize that my inflexibility could stifle the ideas of others and limit my opportunities for growth and development. And so I remain on a constant mission to improve.

Looking for ways to better ourselves is what the opportunity check is all about. We will discuss those improvements further under Compass Principle 8: Creating an Action Plan for Success.

Chapter 4
Removing Hindrances
(Compass Principle 6)

Compass Principle 6
Identify Your Destiny Blockers (Do a Barrier Check)

The next stop on your journey requires you to identify your destiny blockers. I use this term to refer to the diverse things our Enemy, the Devil, uses to prevent Christ-followers from moving forward in our God-given purposes. Examples of destiny blockers include . . .

Destiny Blockers

- Fear
- Abuse
- Addiction
- Hurt
- Rejection
- Comfort

- Negative words
- Negative images
- Negative environments
- Reluctance to forgive
- Abandonment

The roots of most blockers can be traced to things that happened in our pasts. Sometimes these blockers get their start during childhood. Often they are linked to an embarrassing situation we just can't forget. They can also develop as we repeatedly recall an insult—for me, it would be the time a coworker commented that I wasn't leadership material.

While destiny blockers can rise from various problems or issues, they all result in our tendency to remain stagnant in our faith and hesitant to take the calculated risks necessary to move forward in the ways God intends. They lock us in a self-defeating spiral that discourages us from living out what we were created to do.

Be honest with yourself. What are your destiny blockers?

_____

_____

In what ways have you allowed them to prevent you from pursuing your destiny?

_____

_____

Once you know what serves as a barrier between you and a purposeful life, you can create an action plan for dismantling it. Start by identifying a practical resource that may help you overcome your destiny blocker. For example, if your blocker is linked to negative words directed at you during childhood, consider seeing a counselor to help you sort through your feelings. *Don't let stereotypes about counseling prevent you from seeking help.* Counseling is an effective way to overcome destiny blockers.

Next, identify a specific action that counteracts the barrier. For example, the destiny blocker of negative words can be minimized by internalizing positive words or phrases that more accurately describe you. Over time, rehearsing and incorporating positive words in your speech and thoughts will give way to a new, improved perception of who you are in Christ. Similarly, listening to motivational sermons or reading motivational books can help build self-confidence and a healthy self-perception. I'm often motivated by the words of pastor Conway Edwards, but also inspired by the teachings of Bishop T. D. Jakes and Joel Osteen. Know which voices speak life and hope into you, and find ways to incorporate them into your week.

Finally, but most importantly, find Scripture references that dispel your destiny blocker. Statements such as *"you'll never amount to anything"* are nullified as we learn to rely on truths expressed in passages such as Philippians 4:13: *"I can do all things through Christ who strengthens me."*

Before I share a personal destiny blocker and explain how I overcame it, I must warn you about a common blocker many of us fail to identify and defend against. At first glance, "comfort" may seem out of place when I say it belongs with the rest of the blockers mentioned. But the sad truth is that comfort—complacency and doing business as usual in spite of a heart that is eager to move forward—is the most powerful blocker of all.

You see, complacency doesn't mix with a purpose-filled life. It won't improve a situation in which work constantly bleeds into family time or financial concerns keep us awake at night. So if you realize that complacency is a destiny blocker standing in your way, it's time to take leaps of faith to move in a new direction. Moving out of your comfort zone just might solve your problems.

I speak from experience when I say that the rewards of undergoing a spiritual journey toward purposefulness far outweigh the discomfort or stress the effort brings. Similarly, pushing through destiny blockers is worth the labor.

Several years ago I identified my greatest destiny blocker—fear. I had a paralyzing fear of doing anything in front of people since I was a young girl. In one instance, my aunt wanted me to be the flower girl in her wedding. I was so terrified of walking down that aisle that I cried and protested with a vengeance. The thought of everyone's eyes following me as I walked down that bridal path was more than I could bear. As a result, my aunt decided to enlist a younger cousin to be her flower girl instead. My little cousin performed as if she were made for the spotlight, making my meltdown look even more ridiculous.

In college, I earned an internship that forced me to confront this fear. As one of the requirements of the internship, I had to give an oral presentation. Initially, public speaking seemed like a good idea; I was certain it would be my chance to impress others. As the day approached, however, I was so scared of forgetting a key point that I wrote my *entire* speech on a stack of index cards. I even wrote my name on a card in case I forgot that. When it was time for me to speak, I shook so much that I was afraid the audience would wonder if an earthquake had struck under my feet. Only by the grace of God did I manage to get through it.

In case you're thinking people walked up to congratulate me on a good presentation that day or you're assuming that my nerves were all in my mind, you're wrong. My presentation was *terrible!* But the good news is that I was blessed to have a manager who encouraged me in those days despite that dismal performance. At the end of that speech, she had placed a pen set on my desk with a note that read, "Well done." After that, regardless of how I felt about the presentation, I allowed her feedback to give me a sense of accomplishment. It didn't matter that I had stumbled over some words or kept looking at index cards rather than my audience. By simply doing the presentation, I'd taken the first step toward conquering my fear.

In the years to come, I worked hard to overcome that lingering fear of performing tasks in front of people by taking on leadership roles that required me to do just that. I volunteered to lead cross-functional project teams and teach process improvement classes, all of which increased my exposure to group settings. Along the way, I solicited feedback from team members and trainees on my ability to deliver content effectively. This served to lessen my anxiety and build my confidence.

Please know that none of these actions proved easy—especially at first. It took much prayer and practice to follow through on my goals. Over time, however, I began to feel more comfortable presenting in front of crowds. Though I still get nervous today while presenting, a little anxiety is good: it keeps me totally reliant on God's help. Only with his power can I perform with excellence.

Today I give presentations to CEOs and teach coaching seminars to executives, business owners, and large groups. When I was young and too frightened to be a flower girl, I never imagined I'd reach this point. And as a college student, I could only dream of the freedom I now enjoy. But by God's grace, the day came when I not only identified my greatest destiny blocker but also took steps to begin overcoming it.

One of my favorite Scriptures is 2 Timothy 1:7: "For God hath not given us the spirit of fear; but of power, and of love, and of a sound mind" (KJV). To this day I reflect on this Scripture whenever I feel nervous or apprehensive.

God has a calling on your life that exceeds your perceived limitations. Ask him to show you how to move from where you are to where he wants you to be.

Chapter 5
Making a Plan and Executing It
(Compass Principles 7–10)

Compass Principle 7:
Determine Where You Should Be (Do a Dream Check)

It's time to get your dream, a vision for your future, down on paper. Let's do a little reflection on what we've covered so far. Please respond to the following:

1. Would you say that you are currently living a purposeful life? Explain your answer.

_____

_____

_____

2. How would you describe your spiritual foundation? Are you close to God or far from him?

_____

_____

_____

3. On a scale of 1 to 10, with 10 meaning "perfectly" and 1 meaning "not at all," how well does your current job or volunteer position align with your talents and gifts?

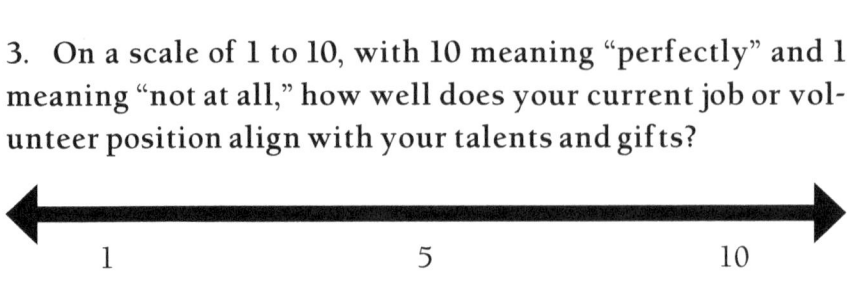

4. Are you using your talents to meet the needs of others? If not, what is the destiny blocker that seems to prevent you from doing so? What's your action plan for removing that barrier?

_____

_____

We've learned about how God has a unique purpose for each of us. We've considered gifts and passions within us that help us discern what type of work he intends we do. If you do not have a clear understanding of what God desires for you, pause and pray. Ask him to give you divine wisdom to identify your unique purpose with grace and humility. Seek his specific will for your life.

What venture do you feel God is impressing on your heart? What's your dream?

_____

_____

Does the idea align with your gifts? Explain.

_____

_____

How might following through on the pursuit of this task help you to bless others?

_____

_____

If you have a clear idea of your purpose, take time to identify incremental steps to move in that direction. Your journey may take months or several years, depending on your God-given role. Be aware that rushing to fulfill your destiny without being fully prepared can be detrimental. Taking your time and accepting that there will be difficulties along the way can save you a lot of heartache.

I find great encouragement in the life story of one of America's greatest entertainers. Do you think Walt Disney immediately came up with feature-length cartoons and dozens of innovative ideas for his billion-dollar theme park, or do you think his success unfolded over time? It took years for this genius to find his way. Early in his career, he was fired by a newspaper editor who felt he had "no imagination" and contributed "no good ideas." After that, he started a number of businesses that ended in bankruptcy and failure.[4] However, Disney didn't lose sight of his lifetime goals. He remained steadfast and eventually found the creative recipes for success. Today, Walt Disney theme parks provide joyous entertainment for individuals of all ages across the world, and his innovative movies are entertaining yet another generation.

If you still feel a bit unsure about just what it is God would have you do with your life, that's okay. Just don't rush the process. Sometimes God has us in a holding pattern until we release certain things or people that could derail our purpose. Sometimes he lovingly withholds answers about the future so that we'll make time for rest and growth. I encourage you to remain in constant prayer regarding your purpose. God will reveal it in time. Make him your focus while you wait.

Once you have a reasonable understanding of where you should be, it's time to expand on the concept. Give that dream permission to grow in scale as you weigh possibilities associated with it. I like to do this through something I term the visioning process.

The visioning process is a technique in which an individual conceptualizes a desired future with imagery, typically using a vision board as a means of cataloging ideas. This tangible record of compelling, vivid images serves as a great motivator to keep a person on the mission of reaching his or her God-given goals.

I encourage the use of images for those looking to transition into a new career path because we often just verbalize our goals and desires, write them down on notepads, and move on without taking action. But by actually *visualizing* our goals and *making physical representations of how we see our destinies unfolding*, we gain a powerful sense of realization that a mere list rarely delivers. And this, I find, is motivating.

Let's consider what is needed in creating your own vision board. Begin by jotting down answers to these questions:

1. What is my major life goal, and when did my desire for it begin?

_____

_____

2. With what gifts or talents has the Lord equipped me that will help me in reaching that goal?

_____

_____

3. Exactly where do I see myself in the future, and what will I do there?

_____

_____

4. What destiny blockers have I overcome? What do I need to overcome to live out my dreams?

_____

_____

5. Who will be positively influenced by me living out my dreams and aspirations? How?

_____

_____

6. What legacy will I leave as a result of my dream becoming a reality?

_____

_____

7. How will my passions and visions bring glory to God?

_____

_____

Now that you have a basic vision and some answers in mind, pause for a supply run. You'll need a poster board, markers, tape or glue, and whatever embellishments you think might make your personal vision board more fun. (Old photos and magazine cutouts are great tools in assembling this aid.)

Here's a peek at a vision board I made years ago that may give you some simple design ideas. As you'll see, it's nothing fancy. Instead, the poster is a clean visual reminder that God has called and equipped me to fulfill a unique purpose.

Vision Board

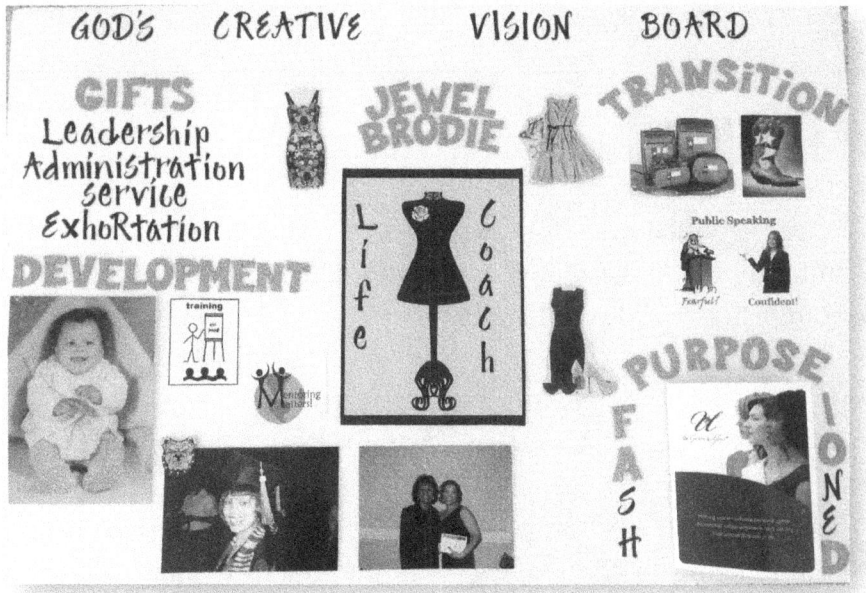

Once you've gathered supplies, turn your poster board into a visual of where you plan to go in the future.

I hope you have conceptualized your future with a vision board of your own. Now, to further solidify your plan, use those visuals as inspiration for writing a purpose affirmation statement. In other words, write down a clear and concise statement that affirms the destiny you believe God has designed for you. I'll give you a couple of examples to get you started:

Example 1: *My purpose is to bring glory to God by equipping men and women with the tools and resources they need to make sound financial decisions. I want to be a financial advisor.*

Example 2: *My purpose is to know Christ intimately, to develop his character in my life, and to make disciples by ministering the Word of God. I want to be a discipleship leader.*

Now it's your turn. What is your purpose affirmation statement?

_____

_____

Congratulations! You are closer to realizing your vision of a fulfilling life. Take a few minutes to add some final touches to your vision board to celebrate.

Compass Principle 8:
Create an Action Plan

The eighth stop on your journey involves creating an action plan to help you effectively walk in purpose from today until you reach your goal. The old Ben Franklin quote still holds true: "If you fail to plan, you plan to fail."[5] So let's guard against inaction.

We know where we are today and where we want to be tomorrow, but *how* we get there is another matter.

For that reason, your action plan should include short and long-term goals. Short-term goals are things you can achieve in the near future, usually within twelve months. These goals, which are often fairly accessible, are great motivators because they provide a sense of accomplishment as you make strides toward a bigger payoff. Short-term goals can include things like taking a skills assessment, enrolling in a financial management class, or volunteering. Steps like these often serve to help us clarify our visions and to prepare us to embrace those visions once they become realities.

Long-term goals are those that normally take a year or more to reach. These can include paying off debt prior to launching a business, graduating from college, or writing a book.

The following table is a sample of an action plan I completed several years ago as I began to work toward becoming a certified Life Purpose Coach®. Notice that my written plan included both short and long-term goals. As I moved toward my goal, I gave myself milestones meant to strengthen my gifts and talents, develop my opportunity areas, overcome my destiny blockers, and help me remain accountable for taking action toward my purpose.

Table 1.0 Action Plan

	Actions	Estimated Completion Date	Status
1	Identify and select a Life Coach training program	09/2009	Complete
2	Begin Life Purpose Coach training	10/2009	Complete
3	Identify a business name	12/2009	Complete
4	Create a business plan for my Life Coach business	01/2010	Complete
5	Begin process of requesting trademark for my business name	01/2010	Complete
6	Identify a resource to create my company logo and website	01/2010	Complete
7	Complete the certification requirements to become a Certified Life Purpose Coach®	07/2010	Complete
8	Identify first speaking engagement as a Certified Life Purpose Coach®	10/2011	Complete

Try creating your own action plan below. Be sure to include both short and long-term items.

Table 2.0

	Actions	Estimated Completion Date	Status
1			
2			
3			
4			
5			
6			

Compass Principle 9: Embrace Purposeful Mentorship

The ninth stop on your journey involves identifying accountability partners and a mentor who can help you stay on track to achieve your dreams. Who can assist and encourage you while holding you to your commitments? Who will want to see you succeed, but will also tell you what you *need* to hear rather than what you *want* to hear? Finding the right people to support you and cheer you on will be critically helpful when you become discouraged or feel yourself sinking in self-doubt.

Keep in mind that your accountability partners and mentors may change. Your first mentor may go through life changes—getting married, having children, moving, or taking on additional responsibilities—that may mean he or she can no longer play an active role in your life. If that happens, don't be discouraged; instead, ask God to provide another accountability partner for you and seek one out in faith.

God has placed several people in my life to encourage and motivate me. One of my former coworkers, who eventually became a close friend, served as my accountability partner as well as a role model. Once I shared my purpose with her, she followed up with me continually to ensure I never lost sight of God's calling on my life. She often inquired about my progression toward operating in purpose, and she shared valuable testimony based on her own journey.

This friend's story was of enormous value as I took steps toward my future. She had been laid off, but rather than seeing the matter as a personal defeat, she used the setback as an opportunity to create her own business called Unhurried Life. Instead of succumbing to self-pity, she made a business plan, completed a ton of action items, and successfully launched her vision. Today she is recognized as one of the top ten organizers in the Dallas-Fort Worth area.[6] Even today, I look to her for advice on my Life Coaching business. She always provides great insight and continues to support and encourage me in my business endeavors.

List three potential accountability partners.
   1.
   2.
   3.

Once you have your vision board, purpose affirmation statement, and action plan in place, make a lunch date with one of the individuals on this accountability partners list. Share your dream for the future, and ask your friend to help you stay focused by checking in with you regularly.

A few years ago, God placed a mentor, Pat Hartman, in my life. I call her my mentor because she was an experienced and trusted advisor who purposefully encouraged me along my journey. She had many years of experience teaching the concepts of purposeful living, and she was well respected by ministry leaders at my church. As you continue your journey toward purpose, identify a mentor to advise you on various aspects of your God-given role. Mentors aren't just cheerleaders or shoulders to cry on. They are often prayer warriors, too.

People frequently tell me they don't know how to find a mentor. It may help to know that when I first met my mentor, I had no clue she would fill that role and provide valuable advice for my business. I first saw her briefly at our church, but we hadn't been formally introduced. A few months later, I saw her again at a department store, but I still didn't know her name. I introduced myself that day before we went our separate ways to browse the aisles. But even then, I saw my mentor-to-be as an acquaintance rather than someone from whom I could learn.

Things changed when the creative director of my church asked me to co-teach a seminar for a women's conference. Accustomed to teaching seminars on my own, I wasn't exactly thrilled with leading a class with a partner (and when I called my assigned partner, she seemed apprehensive as well). But what a delightful surprise awaited us! When we agreed to meet to prepare, I realized my new partner was the woman I'd encountered at the department store. During our meeting, we warmed to each other—and to our church's idea—immediately.

As we finalized the course materials for our seminar, we saw how our strengths complemented each other's. And in the end, we were impressed with how we interacted while teaching. I learned so much from her. She was well versed in God's Word, always incorporated Scriptures into her lesson plans, and often used analogies between biblical references and real life situations to build clarity and understanding for our students. Most importantly, she always stressed that living out her purpose could only be achieved through God's help, because in teaching a class like ours she was operating outside her comfort zone. Her friendship, in little time, became such a blessing to me.

Which individuals come to mind when you consider potential qualities of a good mentor?

_____

_____

Make a dinner date with a friend you feel would be a good mentor to you, or consider asking your pastor for the name of someone who might fill that role. Share your dream for the future with the mentor candidate and ask that individual to help you stay focused through regular check-ins. Ask him or her to pray for you and to encourage you in your walk with the Lord along the way.

When it comes to the topic of accountability partners and mentors, I would be remiss if I didn't take the opportunity to say that my greatest encourager is my husband. Whenever I begin to doubt my purpose, he reaffirms his belief that God's hand is on my life. When I get tired, he finds ways to energize me. If you are unmarried and seeking a mate, one of the most critical items on your checklist for a spouse should be supportiveness; a good spouse is a tremendous gift!

Compass Principle 10: Take the First Step

The last stop on your journey is actually the beginning of your life-changing adventure. Throughout this book, I've given you some tools to identify that great *something* for which you were created—whether it's raising a family or starting a business. And know that I am cheering you on! But now, I must step back and let you begin the task of putting one foot in front of the other as you make your way from today's dreams into the reality of an exciting tomorrow. You must decisively move toward purposeful living. There will never be a "perfect" time to make the changes we've been discussing. That's why it's so important to realize that now is the right time to begin.

In picking up this book, you showed interest in purposeful living and in anchoring your days in wisdom and focus. You demonstrated faith in the fact that the Creator God loves you, has a plan for you, and delights in you seeking his help to pursue your future. And in completing the various checks and creating your vision board and action plan, you jumped the turbulent waves standing between you and a meaningful life that utilizes your gifts and may well serve to bless the world.

So go ahead, step out in faith. Continue your journey in earnest. And know that I'm asking the Lord to bless and encourage you, to buoy you with his love and with the certainty that his purposes for you are great!

> ***"You will never know***
>
> ***what you can achieve***
>
> ***until you take steps***
>
> ***toward what you believe."***
>
> -- Jewel Brodie-Reid

Notes

1. "From Stutterer to Star: How James Earl Jones Found his Voice." Posted October 12, 2014. *PBS News Hour:* http://www.pbs.org/newshour/bb/james-earl-jones-returns-broadway/ (April 15, 2016).
2. Wayne Grudem, *Systematic Theology: An Introduction to Biblical Doctrine.* (Leicester, England: Zondervan, 1994), 1016.
3. "Spiritual Gifts Assessment Tool." LifeWay Articles. *http://www.lifeway.com/Article/Women-Leadership-Spiritual-gifts-growth-service* (April 15, 2016).
4. "50 Famously Successful People Who Failed First." Posted February 16, 2010. *OnlineCollege.org:* http://www.onlinecollege.org/2010/02/16/50-famously-successful-people-who-failed-at-first/ (April 19, 2016).
5. "Ben Franklin Quotes." *GoodReads:* http://www.goodreads.com/quotes/460142-if-you-fail-to-plan-you-are-planning-to-fail (April 20, 2016).
6. In the Dallas area and looking for a professional organizer? Learn more about my friend and accountability partner Michelle Earney at her website: http://unhurriedlife.com.

For Further Reading

Brennfleck, Kevin and Kay Marie. *Live Your Calling: A Practical Guide to Finding and Fulfilling Your Mission in Life* (San Francisco: Jossey-Bass, 2005).

Brazelton, Katie. *Pathway to Purpose for Women* (Grand Rapids, Mich.: Zondervan, 2005).

Jakes, T. D. *Destiny: Step into Your Purpose* (Nashville: FaithWords, 2015).

Meyers, Joyce. *The Root of Rejection: Escape the Bondage of Rejection and Experience the Freedom of God's Acceptance* (Fenton, Mo.: Life in the Word, 1994).

About the Author

Jewel Brodie-Reid is the owner and creator of the independent Life Coach business **The Gem in You**. Jewel is a corporate professional with over 20 years experience in process improvement methods for manufacturing, human resources, healthcare, market research, and education. During her career, she has implemented quality initiatives that saved companies millions of dollars. Jewel's background is diverse, with experiences in global management, engineering, training, and coaching.

As an instructor in process improvement methodology, Jewel quickly discovered a love for coaching, mentoring, and training employees. While Jewel has accomplished much success in her corporate career, her passion is helping women achieve their personal, career, and life goals.

Jewel is a certified Life Purpose Coach® from Life Purpose Coaching Centers International. You may contact Jewel through her website, http://www.thegeminyou.com.

www.ingramcontent.com/pod-product-compliance
Lightning Source LLC
Chambersburg PA
CBHW070801050426
42452CB00012B/2446